MAMA BAT and BABY BAT
Screech, Chirp, Chatter

Copyright © 2025 Lisa Boeglin
Illustrations copyright © 2025 Lisa Boeglin
All Rights Reserved

This is a work of fiction. Names, places, characters and incidents are either the product of the author's imagination or are used fictitiously, and any resemblance to any actual persons, living or dead, businesses, organizations, events or locales is entirely coincidental.

No part of this book may be reproduced or transmitted in any form or by any means, electronic or mechanical, including photocopying, recording, or by any information storage and retrieval system, without permission in writing from the author.

Library of Congress Control Number: 2025912623

Publishing Coordinator – Clarissa Willis
Book Design – Sharon Kizziah-Holmes

SOLANDER PRESS
Springdale, Arkansas

Paperback ISBN: 978-1-966675-22-8
Hardback ISBN: ISBN: 978-1-966675-21-1
eBook ISBN: 978-1-966675-23-5

Dedication

To my second-grade students at McCutchanville and Oak Hill Elementary Schools in Evansville, Indiana—

Thank you for your curiosity, big questions, and willingness to become proud "bat nerds" with me. Learning alongside you was pure joy, and your enthusiasm inspired this book. Thank you for motivating me to cross off a bucket list dream.

MAMA BAT and BABY BAT
Screech, Chirp, Chatter

written by
LISA BOEGLIN

illustrated by
LYNDSI DEER

Hanging upside down,
Mama Bat gives birth,
curves her wing,
and scoops up the

falling

baby.

Cling, clasp, clutch, cradle swaddle and tuck, sip, suck.

A baby bat is called a pup. Most bats only have one baby at a time. However, some bats can have more than one pup.

Mama Bat guides the pup to her chest
to keep him safe and warm.

She cradles him close
to deliver his first drink of milk.

She snuggles him and memorizes his scent.

Bats are mammals. Like all mammals, baby bats get milk from their mother.

sniff, snuff, snuffle

"Screech, chirp, chatter, chatter, screech."
Mama Bat chatters to her clinging baby.

"Screech, chirp, chatter, chatter, screech."
He responds.

Soon, they know each other's voices.

Every bat has a unique voice. As soon as a pup is born, the mother and baby chatter back and forth so they can recognize each other's voice.

flap, flap, flutter

Tucked in tight, Mama Bat carries her baby to the highest point in the cave and secures him to the roof.

Mother bats place their pups on the roof of a cave to keep them safe from predators. Predators are animals that might harm the baby.

Mama Bat leaves the cave.
Her baby remains behind.

Bats are nocturnal animals that sleep during the day and are active at night. Bats search for food at night and can eat up to **1200** bugs an hour. Nursing bats eat even more bugs. Newborn pups don't eat bugs yet, so they stay behind while the mother looks for food for herself.

Crawling on piles of clinging bats,
Baby Bat toddles and wobbles, searching for Mama.
"Screech, chirp, chirp, chatter, chatter, screech."
He cries out for her.

Her scent has disappeared. He wriggles and wiggles, looking for his Mama.

Bats often gather tightly together in caves. Some roost and hibernate in clusters of up to 400 bats per square foot, while others roost more loosely in smaller groups or alone.

"Screech, chirp, chirp, chatter, chatter, screech."
He cries out again.
Mama's voice has vanished.
Has Mama vanished too?
He wriggles and wiggles further.

Climb, creep, crawl.
Baby bat reaches and clutches onto other bats. Losing his grip, he slips. Grasping and groping, he pulls himself up and reattaches to the top of the cave.

Bats have knees that point backward and outward, allowing them to crawl on the walls and ceilings of caves.

Bats crawl on top of the tight clusters when roosting to move around the cave. If a bat falls without reattaching to the wall, it will likely die. Predators wait on the cave floor to eat a falling bat.

Baby Bat wobbles and toddles, searching.

No sight of Mama.   No scent of Mama.

No sound of Mama.

He wriggles and wiggles further.

Bats fly with precision, using echolocation to avoid objects. But when they crawl or walk, it may look clumsy.

As dawn breaks, Mama Bat returns.

Sniff, snuff, snuffle.
Baby Bat's scent has disappeared.
Scanning,
    seeking,
        searching
among the piles of bats,
Mama Bat explores further.

Bats return to their roost after foraging for food. Nursing bats eat about 2 times as many insects as other bats. The additional food is required for the mother bat to produce milk for her pup.

"Screech, chirp, chirp, chatter, chatter, screech."
She calls out to her baby.

"Screech, chirp, chirp, chatter, chatter screech."
He responds.

Following Mama Bat's chattering, Baby Bat climbs, creeps, and crawls toward Mama's voice.

Bats use their scent and voice to identify their pups. Each bat has its own unique scent and voice.

A faint scent is present.

She calls out again.

Baby Bat responds.

Reunited, Mama Bat caresses and strokes the top of Baby Bat's head with her muzzle.

"Screech, chirp, chirp, chatter, chatter, screech."

"Screech, chirp, chirp, chatter, chatter, screech."

Mama Bat chatters, reassuring her pup she is still with him.

Bats are protective of their pups and show affection by cuddling their baby.

cling, clasp, clutch, cradle

swaddle and tuck,
sip, suck

Cling, clasp, clutch, cradle, swaddle and tuck, sip, suck.

Mama Bat clings to the roof, nestled with her pup.

Snug and secure, they close their eyes and sleep.

Baby bats cling to their mother by hanging onto her waist with their toes.

Author's Note

Several years ago, my second-grade students became fascinated by bats. As we dove into research together, we discovered that many bat species are endangered. Threatened by factors like habitat loss, pesticide use, and a devastating disease called White-Nose Syndrome, my students were eager to help. Over time, they raised money for bat conservation groups and even became "Batty Baristas," selling coffee and hot drinks to our school staff. With their earnings, they installed a bat house on our school campus.

Learning alongside them, I developed a deep appreciation for these incredible creatures—a fascination that soon became a passion. Today, my students and I proudly call ourselves "Bat Nerds."

That passion took flight when I had the opportunity to visit Bracken Cave, just outside San Antonio, Texas. Home to the largest bat colony in the world, Bracken Cave becomes a nursery each spring, sheltering around 20 million Mexican free-tailed bats and their pups. Watching millions of bats pour from the cave at dusk was a breathtaking, unforgettable experience.

Bats are often misunderstood but play a vital role in our ecosystems. I wanted to write a story showing their gentle, nurturing side, inspiring readers to care for and protect the world's only flying mammals.

Many people think they know all about bats, but not all of it is true! These are called myths. Let's look at some common bat myths and dig into the facts.

Myths Busted

Bats are blind. BUSTED! Bats' eyes are fine. They see as well as any other animal. However, bats use echolocation to send out sound waves and listen for the echo to hunt for food.
All bats carry rabies. BUSTED! According to the U.S. Centers for Disease Control and Prevention, only 5% to 6% of bats captured for testing have rabies. Therefore, you shouldn't handle a bat just like any other wildlife.
Bats fly toward people and get tangled in their hair to build a nest. BUSTED! Using echolocation, bats might fly erratically and swoop down on you, but they are tracking the movement of bugs. Bats don't make nests, so they aren't looking to get into your hair.
Bats suck people's blood. BUSTED! While vampire bats have been known to bite people on rare occasions, they feed on cattle and other animals. They make a small bite and suck a tiny amount of blood. The animals don't even feel it, and it doesn't harm the animals.
Bats aren't crucial to the planet. BUSTED! Bats eat thousands of bugs, including pesky mosquitoes, each night, providing natural pest control for plants. Bats are pollinators. They also spread seeds that grow into plants.
Bats are a type of bird. BUSTED! Bats are the only flying mammals on the planet. They have fur, give live births, and mothers nurse their young.

Sensory Language Glossary

Word	Meaning
sniff, snuff, snuffle	The sniffing sounds a bat makes to recognize a scent.
screech, chirp, chatter	Sounds used by a bat to communicate.
Cling, clasp, clutch, cradle.	The ways a pup holds on to its mother while she holds it next to herself.

How You Can Help

- If you find a bat in your home, call animal control or wildlife experts to remove and/or relocate the animal safely.
- If you find an injured bat, contact wildlife experts to rehabilitate the animal.
- Provide natural habitats for bats. If it is not a hazard, leave dead or dying trees for bats to use as roosting sites.
- Avoid disturbing bats. Stay out of caves and mines where bats are hibernating for the winter. Disturbing their hibernation places their life at risk.
- Plant a pollinator garden for bats. Bats are pollinators for various night-blooming plants in the western United States. As they feed on the nectar of these plants, they pollinate others.
- Create a bat-friendly habitat. Creating a space with native plants will ensure a food source for bats. Native plants attract more insects, which are the favorite food of most bats in the US.
- Reduce pesticides. Bats eat thousands of insects each day.
- Place a bat house on your property. Bat houses should be placed out of the reach of predators such as cats, skunks, and snakes. Don't place a bat house on a tree. Instead, attach it to a building or a 10–15 foot pole. Consult experts for the best design for your location.
- Become a "Bat Ambassador". Learn about the benefits of bats so you can educate others and dispel myths.
- Donate to organizations like Bat Conservation International that protect bats and their habitats.

About the Author

Lisa is a former Indiana Teacher of the Year, a lover of nature, an artist, a traveler, and a proud self-proclaimed bat nerd. A history enthusiast and storyteller at heart, she now lives in southern Indiana with her husband and their rotten fur baby. She's the proud mom of four adult children and "BeeBee" to two precious grandchildren.

From the moment she began reading picture books aloud to her students, Lisa dreamed of seeing her name on a cover, bringing stories to life for young readers everywhere.

As a retired elementary teacher with a master's degree in Early Childhood Education, Lisa continues to inspire future educators by being an adjunct instructor at a local community college. She's led professional development sessions for teachers at the local, state, regional, and national levels. When she's not writing or spending time with her grandkids, you'll find her exploring new places, wandering through gardens, or tucked away in her Evansville home, crafting picture books filled with heart, history, and wonder.

About the Illustrator

Some of her earliest memories are of drawing and painting, so Lyndsi Deer is an artist and creative at heart. She loves to experiment with new media and dabbles in all kinds of creative endeavors, ranging from illustration to murals. Although she's been creative her whole life, she spent over 13 years working as a registered nurse and earned her Master's degree in nursing in 2015. She felt called to pursue her art as a career in 2021 and hasn't looked back!

Although she's often covered in paint, Lyndsi's most important job is being a wife and mama to three busy and amazing kiddos (two fluffy cats and two goldfish!). She loves Jesus, spending time with her family and friends, the sunshine, and lots of color. She resides in Evansville, IN, where she juggles all the fun of family and art.

www.ingramcontent.com/pod-product-compliance
Lightning Source LLC
Chambersburg PA
CBRC091205010526
44107CB00021B/1250